DEAL OR NO DEAL

Scratch & Play

D0167654

STERLING

New York / London

www.sterlingpublishing.com

Deal or No Deal TM & © 2007 by Endemol International B.V.

STERLING and the distinctive Sterling logo are registered trademarks of
Sterling Publishing Co., Inc.

NBC and the NBC peacock logo are registered trademarks of
NBC Universal, Inc.

4   6   8   10   9   7   5

Published by Sterling Publishing Co., Inc.
387 Park Avenue South, New York, NY 10016
© 2007 by Endemol International B.V.
Distributed in Canada by Sterling Publishing
c/o Canadian Manda Group, 165 Dufferin Street
Toronto, Ontario, Canada M6K 3H6
Distributed in the United Kingdom by GMC Distribution Services
Castle Place, 166 High Street, Lewes, East Sussex, England BN7 1XU
Distributed in Australia by Capricorn Link (Australia) Pty. Ltd.
P.O. Box 704, Windsor, NSW 2756, Australia

Printed in China
All rights reserved

Sterling ISBN-13: 978-1-4027-4815-8
ISBN-10: 1-4027-4815-9

For information about custom editions, special sales, premium and
corporate purchases, please contact Sterling Special Sales
Department at 800-805-5489 or specialsales@sterlingpub.com.

INTRODUCTION

It's easy to play Deal or No Deal Scratch & Play. Each of the two-page spreads is one game. There are 26 briefcases, and they contain the 26 values shown in the Deal or No Deal box at the bottom of the right page. You are assigned a briefcase at the top of the left page. Don't open it! To start the game, open the six briefcases below it by scratching off the silver coating. Underneath will be six dollar values. Remove these values from the Deal or No Deal box (since no value appears more than once). Then scratch off the bank offer. Now it's time to make a decision: Deal or No Deal?

If you accept the deal, then the game is over and you've won the amount of the deal. If not, then you continue on, scratching off more cases until you either accept a deal, or reach the final case on the right page. At that point you have the option of switching your original case with the final one. Choose one and scratch it off. That is your prize.

(Note that the prize money is totally fake. Don't get too excited if you hit the $1,000,000 jackpot.)

For the competitive among you, get two copies of the book and have the two players play the same game. The values are the same, so the person who ends up with less money can't blame anything on luck.

Here is your case: **DON'T OPEN IT!**

Start by opening these six cases:

$400 $500 $50 $25 $25,000 $300

The bank offer is:
$40,000

If **NO DEAL**, continue by opening these five cases:

$75,000 $750 $100 $100,000 $10,000

The bank offer is:
$80,000

If **NO DEAL**, continue by opening these four cases:

$75 $50,000 $200,000 $1,000

The bank offer is:
$131,000

If **NO DEAL**, continue by opening these three cases:

$10 $5 $750,000

The bank offer is:
$176,000

If **NO DEAL**, continue by opening these two cases:

$1,000,000 $0.01

The bank offer is: $123,000

DEAL or **NO DEAL**

If **NO DEAL**, continue by opening this case:

$500,000

The bank offer is: $145,000

DEAL or **NO DEAL**

If **NO DEAL**, continue by opening this case:

$200

The bank offer is: $172,000

DEAL or **NO DEAL**

If **NO DEAL**, continue by opening this case:

$5,000

The bank offer is: $238,000

DEAL or **NO DEAL**

If **NO DEAL**, continue by opening this case:

$400,000

The bank offer is: $153,000

DEAL or **NO DEAL**

If **NO DEAL**, there are just two cases left. You can keep your original case or switch to the one at right. Choose one and open it.

$300,000

DEAL or **NO DEAL**

$		$	
$	.01	$	1,000
$	1	$	5,000
$	5	$	10,000
$	10	$	25,000
$	25	$	50,000
$	50	$	75,000
$	75	$	100,000
$	100	$	200,000
$	200	$	300,000
$	300	$	400,000
$	400	$	500,000
$	500	$	750,000
$	750	$	1,000,000

Here is your case: **DON'T OPEN IT!**

Start by opening these six cases:

The bank offer is:

If **NO DEAL**, continue by opening these five cases:

The bank offer is:

If **NO DEAL**, continue by opening these four cases:

The bank offer is:

If **NO DEAL**, continue by opening these three cases:

The bank offer is:

If **NO DEAL**, continue by opening these two cases:

The bank offer is: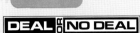

DEAL or NO DEAL

If **NO DEAL**, continue by opening this case:

The bank offer is:

DEAL or NO DEAL

If **NO DEAL**, continue by opening this case:

The bank offer is:

DEAL or NO DEAL

If **NO DEAL**, continue by opening this case:

The bank offer is:

DEAL or NO DEAL

If **NO DEAL**, continue by opening this case:

The bank offer is:

DEAL or NO DEAL

If **NO DEAL**, there are just two cases left. You can keep your original case or switch to the one at right. Choose one and open it.

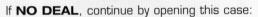

DEAL or NO DEAL	
$ .01	$ 1,000
$ 1	$ 5,000
$ 5	$ 10,000
$ 10	$ 25,000
$ 25	$ 50,000
$ 50	$ 75,000
$ 75	$ 100,000
$ 100	$ 200,000
$ 200	$ 300,000
$ 300	$ 400,000
$ 400	$ 500,000
$ 500	$ 750,000
$ 750	$ 1,000,000

Here is your case: **DON'T OPEN IT!**

Start by opening these six cases:

$500,000

The bank offer is:

If **NO DEAL**, continue by opening these five cases:

The bank offer is:

If **NO DEAL**, continue by opening these four cases:

The bank offer is:

If **NO DEAL**, continue by opening these three cases:

The bank offer is:

If **NO DEAL**, continue by opening these two cases:

DEAL NO DEAL Scratch & Play

The bank offer is:

DEAL or NO DEAL

If **NO DEAL**, continue by opening this case:

The bank offer is:

DEAL or NO DEAL

If **NO DEAL**, continue by opening this case:

The bank offer is:

DEAL or NO DEAL

If **NO DEAL**, continue by opening this case:

The bank offer is:

DEAL or NO DEAL

If **NO DEAL**, continue by opening this case:

The bank offer is:

DEAL or NO DEAL

If **NO DEAL**, there are just two cases left. You can keep your original case or switch to the one at right. Choose one and open it.

DEAL or NO DEAL	
$ .01	$ 1,000
$ 1	$ 5,000
$ 5	$ 10,000
$ 10	$ 25,000
$ 25	$ 50,000
$ 50	$ 75,000
$ 75	$ 100,000
$ 100	$ 200,000
$ 200	$ 300,000
$ 300	$ 400,000
$ 400	$ 500,000
$ 500	$ 750,000
$ 750	$ 1,000,000

Here is your case: **DON'T OPEN IT!**

Start by opening these six cases:

The bank offer is:

If **NO DEAL**, continue by opening these five cases:

The bank offer is:

If **NO DEAL**, continue by opening these four cases:

The bank offer is:

If **NO DEAL**, continue by opening these three cases:

The bank offer is:

If **NO DEAL**, continue by opening these two cases:

The bank offer is:

DEAL or **NO DEAL**

If **NO DEAL**, continue by opening this case:

The bank offer is: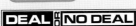

DEAL or **NO DEAL**

If **NO DEAL**, continue by opening this case:

The bank offer is: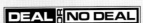

DEAL or **NO DEAL**

If **NO DEAL**, continue by opening this case:

The bank offer is:

DEAL or **NO DEAL**

If **NO DEAL**, continue by opening this case:

The bank offer is:

DEAL or **NO DEAL**

If **NO DEAL**, there are just two cases left. You can keep your original case or switch to the one at right. Choose one and open it.

DEAL or NO DEAL

$		$	
$	.01	$	1,000
$	1	$	5,000
$	5	$	10,000
$	10	$	25,000
$	25	$	50,000
$	50	$	75,000
$	75	$	100,000
$	100	$	200,000
$	200	$	300,000
$	300	$	400,000
$	400	$	500,000
$	500	$	750,000
$	750	$	1,000,000

Here is your case: **DON'T OPEN IT!**

Start by opening these six cases:

The bank offer is: **DEAL ⅊ NO DEAL**

If **NO DEAL**, continue by opening these five cases:

The bank offer is: **DEAL ⅊ NO DEAL**

If **NO DEAL**, continue by opening these four cases:

The bank offer is: **DEAL ⅊ NO DEAL**

If **NO DEAL**, continue by opening these three cases:

The bank offer is: **DEAL ⅊ NO DEAL**

If **NO DEAL**, continue by opening these two cases:

The bank offer is:

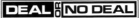

If **NO DEAL**, continue by opening this case:

The bank offer is:

If **NO DEAL**, continue by opening this case:

The bank offer is:

DEAL or NO DEAL

If **NO DEAL**, continue by opening this case:

The bank offer is:

DEAL or NO DEAL

If **NO DEAL**, continue by opening this case:

The bank offer is:

DEAL or NO DEAL

If **NO DEAL**, there are just two cases left. You can keep your original case or switch to the one at right. Choose one and open it.

DEAL or NO DEAL	
$ .01	$ 1,000
$ 1	$ 5,000
$ 5	$ 10,000
$ 10	$ 25,000
$ 25	$ 50,000
$ 50	$ 75,000
$ 75	$ 100,000
$ 100	$ 200,000
$ 200	$ 300,000
$ 300	$ 400,000
$ 400	$ 500,000
$ 500	$ 750,000
$ 750	$ 1,000,000

Here is your case: **DON'T OPEN IT!**

Start by opening these six cases:

The bank offer is:

If **NO DEAL**, continue by opening these five cases:

The bank offer is:

If **NO DEAL**, continue by opening these four cases:

The bank offer is:

If **NO DEAL**, continue by opening these three cases:

The bank offer is:

If **NO DEAL**, continue by opening these two cases:

The bank offer is:

DEAL or NO DEAL

If **NO DEAL**, continue by opening this case:

The bank offer is:

DEAL or NO DEAL

If **NO DEAL**, continue by opening this case:

The bank offer is:

DEAL or NO DEAL

If **NO DEAL**, continue by opening this case:

The bank offer is:

DEAL or NO DEAL

If **NO DEAL**, continue by opening this case:

The bank offer is:

DEAL or NO DEAL

If **NO DEAL**, there are just two cases left. You can keep your original case or switch to the one at right. Choose one and open it.

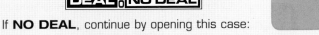

DEAL or	NO DEAL
$ .01	$ 1,000
$ 1	$ 5,000
$ 5	$ 10,000
$ 10	$ 25,000
$ 25	$ 50,000
$ 50	$ 75,000
$ 75	$ 100,000
$ 100	$ 200,000
$ 200	$ 300,000
$ 300	$ 400,000
$ 400	$ 500,000
$ 500	$ 750,000
$ 750	$ 1,000,000

Here is your case: **DON'T OPEN IT!**

Start by opening these six cases:

The bank offer is: **DEAL or NO DEAL**

If **NO DEAL**, continue by opening these five cases:

The bank offer is: **DEAL or NO DEAL**

If **NO DEAL**, continue by opening these four cases:

The bank offer is: **DEAL or NO DEAL**

If **NO DEAL**, continue by opening these three cases:

The bank offer is: **DEAL or NO DEAL**

If **NO DEAL**, continue by opening these two cases:

The bank offer is:

 DEAL or NO DEAL

If **NO DEAL**, continue by opening this case:

The bank offer is:

 DEAL or NO DEAL

If **NO DEAL**, continue by opening this case:

The bank offer is:

DEAL or NO DEAL

If **NO DEAL**, continue by opening this case:

The bank offer is:

 DEAL or NO DEAL

If **NO DEAL**, continue by opening this case:

The bank offer is:

 DEAL or NO DEAL

If **NO DEAL**, there are just two cases left. You can keep your original case or switch to the one at right. Choose one and open it.

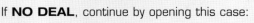

DEAL or	NO DEAL
$ .01	$ 1,000
$ 1	$ 5,000
$ 5	$ 10,000
$ 10	$ 25,000
$ 25	$ 50,000
$ 50	$ 75,000
$ 75	$ 100,000
$ 100	$ 200,000
$ 200	$ 300,000
$ 300	$ 400,000
$ 400	$ 500,000
$ 500	$ 750,000
$ 750	$ 1,000,000

Here is your case: **DON'T OPEN IT!**

Start by opening these six cases:

 $25,000 $5 $10 $1,000,000 $75 $400,000

The bank offer is:

 DEAL☷**NO DEAL**

If **NO DEAL**, continue by opening these five cases:

 $200 $0.01 $300,000 $5,000  $50,000

The bank offer is:

 **DEAL**☷**NO DEAL**

If **NO DEAL**, continue by opening these four cases:

 $400 $50 $1 $300

The bank offer is:

 DEAL☷**NO DEAL**

If **NO DEAL**, continue by opening these three cases:

 $25 $500 $75,000

The bank offer is:

 **DEAL**☷**NO DEAL**

If **NO DEAL**, continue by opening these two cases:

 $100,000 $500,000

The bank offer is: $125,000

DEAL or **NO DEAL**

If **NO DEAL**, continue by opening this case:

The bank offer is: $183,000

DEAL or **NO DEAL**

If **NO DEAL**, continue by opening this case:

The bank offer is: $200,000

DEAL or **NO DEAL**

If **NO DEAL**, continue by opening this case:

The bank offer is: $258,000

DEAL or **NO DEAL**

If **NO DEAL**, continue by opening this case:

The bank offer is: $344,000

DEAL or **NO DEAL**

If **NO DEAL**, there are just two cases left. You can keep your original case or switch to the one at right. Choose one and open it.

DEAL or NO DEAL	
$ .01	$ 1,000
$ 1	$ 5,000
$ 5	$ 10,000
$ 10	$ 25,000
$ 25	$ 50,000
$ 50	$ 75,000
$ 75	$ 100,000
$ 100	$ 200,000
$ 200	$ 300,000
$ 300	$ 400,000
$ 400	$ 500,000
$ 500	$ 750,000
$ 750	$ 1,000,000

Here is your case: **DON'T OPEN IT!**

Start by opening these six cases:

The bank offer is:

If **NO DEAL**, continue by opening these five cases:

The bank offer is:

If **NO DEAL**, continue by opening these four cases:

The bank offer is:

If **NO DEAL**, continue by opening these three cases:

The bank offer is:

If **NO DEAL**, continue by opening these two cases:

The bank offer is:

DEAL or **NO DEAL**

If **NO DEAL**, continue by opening this case:

The bank offer is:

DEAL or **NO DEAL**

If **NO DEAL**, continue by opening this case:

The bank offer is:

DEAL or **NO DEAL**

If **NO DEAL**, continue by opening this case:

The bank offer is:

DEAL or **NO DEAL**

If **NO DEAL**, continue by opening this case:

The bank offer is:

DEAL or **NO DEAL**

If **NO DEAL**, there are just two cases left. You can keep your original case or switch to the one at right. Choose one and open it.

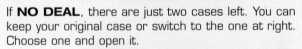

DEAL or **NO DEAL**

$ .01	$ 1,000
$ 1	$ 5,000
$ 5	$ 10,000
$ 10	$ 25,000
$ 25	$ 50,000
$ 50	$ 75,000
$ 75	$ 100,000
$ 100	$ 200,000
$ 200	$ 300,000
$ 300	$ 400,000
$ 400	$ 500,000
$ 500	$ 750,000
$ 750	$ 1,000,000

Here is your case: **DON'T OPEN IT!**

Start by opening these six cases:

The bank offer is:  DEAL or NO DEAL

If **NO DEAL**, continue by opening these five cases:

The bank offer is:  DEAL or NO DEAL

If **NO DEAL**, continue by opening these four cases:

The bank offer is:  DEAL or NO DEAL

If **NO DEAL**, continue by opening these three cases:

The bank offer is:  DEAL or NO DEAL

If **NO DEAL**, continue by opening these two cases:

The bank offer is:

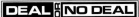

 DEAL or **NO DEAL**

If **NO DEAL**, continue by opening this case:

The bank offer is:

DEAL or **NO DEAL**

If **NO DEAL**, continue by opening this case:

The bank offer is:

DEAL or **NO DEAL**

If **NO DEAL**, continue by opening this case:

The bank offer is:

 **DEAL** or **NO DEAL**

If **NO DEAL**, continue by opening this case:

The bank offer is:

DEAL or **NO DEAL**

If **NO DEAL**, there are just two cases left. You can keep your original case or switch to the one at right. Choose one and open it.

DEAL or NO DEAL	
$ .01	$ 1,000
$ 1	$ 5,000
$ 5	$ 10,000
$ 10	$ 25,000
$ 25	$ 50,000
$ 50	$ 75,000
$ 75	$ 100,000
$ 100	$ 200,000
$ 200	$ 300,000
$ 300	$ 400,000
$ 400	$ 500,000
$ 500	$ 750,000
$ 750	$ 1,000,000

Here is your case: **DON'T OPEN IT!**

Start by opening these six cases:

The bank offer is:

If **NO DEAL**, continue by opening these five cases:

The bank offer is:

If **NO DEAL**, continue by opening these four cases:

The bank offer is:

If **NO DEAL**, continue by opening these three cases:

The bank offer is:

If **NO DEAL**, continue by opening these two cases:

The bank offer is:

DEAL or **NO DEAL**

If **NO DEAL**, continue by opening this case:

The bank offer is:

DEAL or **NO DEAL**

If **NO DEAL**, continue by opening this case:

The bank offer is:

DEAL or **NO DEAL**

If **NO DEAL**, continue by opening this case:

The bank offer is:

DEAL or **NO DEAL**

If **NO DEAL**, continue by opening this case:

The bank offer is:

DEAL or **NO DEAL**

If **NO DEAL**, there are just two cases left. You can keep your original case or switch to the one at right. Choose one and open it.

DEAL or **NO DEAL**

$		$	
$	.01	$	1,000
$	1	$	5,000
$	5	$	10,000
$	10	$	25,000
$	25	$	50,000
$	50	$	75,000
$	75	$	100,000
$	100	$	200,000
$	200	$	300,000
$	300	$	400,000
$	400	$	500,000
$	500	$	750,000
$	750	$	1,000,000

Here is your case: **DON'T OPEN IT!**

Start by opening these six cases:

The bank offer is:

 **DEAL** or **NO DEAL**

If **NO DEAL**, continue by opening these five cases:

The bank offer is:

 **DEAL** or **NO DEAL**

If **NO DEAL**, continue by opening these four cases:

The bank offer is:

 **DEAL** or **NO DEAL**

If **NO DEAL**, continue by opening these three cases:

The bank offer is:

 **DEAL** or **NO DEAL**

If **NO DEAL**, continue by opening these two cases:

The bank offer is:

DEAL or **NO DEAL**

If **NO DEAL**, continue by opening this case:

The bank offer is:

DEAL or **NO DEAL**

If **NO DEAL**, continue by opening this case:

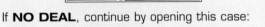

The bank offer is:

DEAL or **NO DEAL**

If **NO DEAL**, continue by opening this case:

The bank offer is:

DEAL or **NO DEAL**

If **NO DEAL**, continue by opening this case:

The bank offer is:

DEAL or **NO DEAL**

If **NO DEAL**, there are just two cases left. You can keep your original case or switch to the one at right. Choose one and open it.

DEAL or **NO DEAL**	
$ .01	$ 1,000
$ 1	$ 5,000
$ 5	$ 10,000
$ 10	$ 25,000
$ 25	$ 50,000
$ 50	$ 75,000
$ 75	$ 100,000
$ 100	$ 200,000
$ 200	$ 300,000
$ 300	$ 400,000
$ 400	$ 500,000
$ 500	$ 750,000
$ 750	$ 1,000,000

Here is your case: **DON'T OPEN IT!**

Start by opening these six cases:

The bank offer is:

If **NO DEAL**, continue by opening these five cases:

The bank offer is:

If **NO DEAL**, continue by opening these four cases:

The bank offer is:

If **NO DEAL**, continue by opening these three cases:

The bank offer is:

If **NO DEAL**, continue by opening these two cases:

The bank offer is: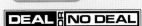

If **NO DEAL**, continue by opening this case:

The bank offer is:

If **NO DEAL**, continue by opening this case:

The bank offer is: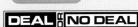

If **NO DEAL**, continue by opening this case:

The bank offer is:

If **NO DEAL**, continue by opening this case:

The bank offer is:

If **NO DEAL**, there are just two cases left. You can keep your original case or switch to the one at right. Choose one and open it.

DEAL 양 NO DEAL		
$ .01	$ 1,000	
$ 1	$ 5,000	
$ 5	$ 10,000	
$ 10	$ 25,000	
$ 25	$ 50,000	
$ 50	$ 75,000	
$ 75	$ 100,000	
$ 100	$ 200,000	
$ 200	$ 300,000	
$ 300	$ 400,000	
$ 400	$ 500,000	
$ 500	$ 750,000	
$ 750	$ 1,000,000	

Here is your case: **DON'T OPEN IT!**

Start by opening these six cases:

The bank offer is:

If **NO DEAL**, continue by opening these five cases:

The bank offer is:

If **NO DEAL**, continue by opening these four cases:

The bank offer is:

If **NO DEAL**, continue by opening these three cases:

The bank offer is:

If **NO DEAL**, continue by opening these two cases:

The bank offer is:

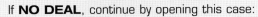

DEAL or NO DEAL

If **NO DEAL**, continue by opening this case:

The bank offer is:

DEAL or NO DEAL

If **NO DEAL**, continue by opening this case:

The bank offer is:

DEAL or NO DEAL

If **NO DEAL**, continue by opening this case:

The bank offer is:

DEAL or NO DEAL

If **NO DEAL**, continue by opening this case:

The bank offer is:

DEAL or NO DEAL

If **NO DEAL**, there are just two cases left. You can keep your original case or switch to the one at right. Choose one and open it.

DEAL or NO DEAL

$		$	
$	.01	$	1,000
$	1	$	5,000
$	5	$	10,000
$	10	$	25,000
$	25	$	50,000
$	50	$	75,000
$	75	$	100,000
$	100	$	200,000
$	200	$	300,000
$	300	$	400,000
$	400	$	500,000
$	500	$	750,000
$	750	$	1,000,000

Here is your case: **DON'T OPEN IT!**

Start by opening these six cases:

The bank offer is:

If **NO DEAL**, continue by opening these five cases:

The bank offer is:

If **NO DEAL**, continue by opening these four cases:

The bank offer is:

If **NO DEAL**, continue by opening these three cases:

The bank offer is:

If **NO DEAL**, continue by opening these two cases:

The bank offer is:

DEAL or **NO DEAL**

If **NO DEAL**, continue by opening this case:

The bank offer is:

DEAL or **NO DEAL**

If **NO DEAL**, continue by opening this case:

The bank offer is:

DEAL or **NO DEAL**

If **NO DEAL**, continue by opening this case:

The bank offer is:

DEAL or **NO DEAL**

If **NO DEAL**, continue by opening this case:

The bank offer is:

DEAL or **NO DEAL**

If **NO DEAL**, there are just two cases left. You can keep your original case or switch to the one at right. Choose one and open it.

DEAL or **NO DEAL**

$		$	
$	.01	$	1,000
$	1	$	5,000
$	5	$	10,000
$	10	$	25,000
$	25	$	50,000
$	50	$	75,000
$	75	$	100,000
$	100	$	200,000
$	200	$	300,000
$	300	$	400,000
$	400	$	500,000
$	500	$	750,000
$	750	$	1,000,000

Here is your case: **DON'T OPEN IT!**

Start by opening these six cases:

The bank offer is:

If **NO DEAL**, continue by opening these five cases:

The bank offer is:

If **NO DEAL**, continue by opening these four cases:

The bank offer is:

If **NO DEAL**, continue by opening these three cases:

The bank offer is:

If **NO DEAL**, continue by opening these two cases:

The bank offer is: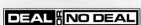

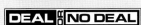

DEAL or NO DEAL

If **NO DEAL**, continue by opening this case:

The bank offer is:

DEAL or NO DEAL

If **NO DEAL**, continue by opening this case:

The bank offer is:

DEAL or NO DEAL

If **NO DEAL**, continue by opening this case:

The bank offer is:

DEAL or NO DEAL

If **NO DEAL**, continue by opening this case:

The bank offer is:

DEAL or NO DEAL

If **NO DEAL**, there are just two cases left. You can keep your original case or switch to the one at right. Choose one and open it.

DEAL or NO DEAL

$ .01	$ 1,000
$ 1	$ 5,000
$ 5	$ 10,000
$ 10	$ 25,000
$ 25	$ 50,000
$ 50	$ 75,000
$ 75	$ 100,000
$ 100	$ 200,000
$ 200	$ 300,000
$ 300	$ 400,000
$ 400	$ 500,000
$ 500	$ 750,000
$ 750	$ 1,000,000

Here is your case: **DON'T OPEN IT!**

Start by opening these six cases:

The bank offer is:

If **NO DEAL**, continue by opening these five cases:

The bank offer is:

If **NO DEAL**, continue by opening these four cases:

The bank offer is:

If **NO DEAL**, continue by opening these three cases:

The bank offer is:

If **NO DEAL**, continue by opening these two cases:

The bank offer is:

DEAL or **NO DEAL**

If **NO DEAL**, continue by opening this case:

The bank offer is: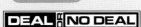

DEAL or **NO DEAL**

If **NO DEAL**, continue by opening this case:

The bank offer is:

DEAL or **NO DEAL**

If **NO DEAL**, continue by opening this case:

The bank offer is:

DEAL or **NO DEAL**

If **NO DEAL**, continue by opening this case:

The bank offer is: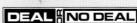

DEAL or **NO DEAL**

If **NO DEAL**, there are just two cases left. You can keep your original case or switch to the one at right. Choose one and open it.

DEAL or NO DEAL	
$ .01	$ 1,000
$ 1	$ 5,000
$ 5	$ 10,000
$ 10	$ 25,000
$ 25	$ 50,000
$ 50	$ 75,000
$ 75	$ 100,000
$ 100	$ 200,000
$ 200	$ 300,000
$ 300	$ 400,000
$ 400	$ 500,000
$ 500	$ 750,000
$ 750	$ 1,000,000

Here is your case: **DON'T OPEN IT!**

Start by opening these six cases:

The bank offer is:

 **DEAL** or **NO DEAL**

If **NO DEAL**, continue by opening these five cases:

The bank offer is:

 **DEAL** or **NO DEAL**

If **NO DEAL**, continue by opening these four cases:

The bank offer is:

 **DEAL** or **NO DEAL**

If **NO DEAL**, continue by opening these three cases:

The bank offer is:

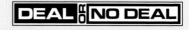 **DEAL** or **NO DEAL**

If **NO DEAL**, continue by opening these two cases:

The bank offer is:

DEAL or NO DEAL

If **NO DEAL**, continue by opening this case:

The bank offer is:

DEAL or NO DEAL

If **NO DEAL**, continue by opening this case:

The bank offer is:

DEAL or NO DEAL

If **NO DEAL**, continue by opening this case:

The bank offer is:

DEAL or NO DEAL

If **NO DEAL**, continue by opening this case:

The bank offer is:

DEAL or NO DEAL

If **NO DEAL**, there are just two cases left. You can keep your original case or switch to the one at right. Choose one and open it.

DEAL or NO DEAL	
$ .01	$ 1,000
$ 1	$ 5,000
$ 5	$ 10,000
$ 10	$ 25,000
$ 25	$ 50,000
$ 50	$ 75,000
$ 75	$ 100,000
$ 100	$ 200,000
$ 200	$ 300,000
$ 300	$ 400,000
$ 400	$ 500,000
$ 500	$ 750,000
$ 750	$ 1,000,000

Here is your case: **DON'T OPEN IT!**

Start by opening these six cases:

The bank offer is:

If **NO DEAL**, continue by opening these five cases:

The bank offer is:

If **NO DEAL**, continue by opening these four cases:

The bank offer is:

If **NO DEAL**, continue by opening these three cases:

The bank offer is:

If **NO DEAL**, continue by opening these two cases:

The bank offer is:

DEAL or **NO DEAL**

If **NO DEAL**, continue by opening this case:

The bank offer is: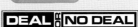

DEAL or **NO DEAL**

If **NO DEAL**, continue by opening this case:

The bank offer is:

DEAL or **NO DEAL**

If **NO DEAL**, continue by opening this case:

The bank offer is:

DEAL or **NO DEAL**

If **NO DEAL**, continue by opening this case:

The bank offer is:

DEAL or **NO DEAL**

If **NO DEAL**, there are just two cases left. You can keep your original case or switch to the one at right. Choose one and open it.

DEAL or **NO DEAL**	
$ .01	$ 1,000
$ 1	$ 5,000
$ 5	$ 10,000
$ 10	$ 25,000
$ 25	$ 50,000
$ 50	$ 75,000
$ 75	$ 100,000
$ 100	$ 200,000
$ 200	$ 300,000
$ 300	$ 400,000
$ 400	$ 500,000
$ 500	$ 750,000
$ 750	$ 1,000,000

Here is your case: **DON'T OPEN IT!**

Start by opening these six cases:

The bank offer is:

If **NO DEAL**, continue by opening these five cases:

The bank offer is:

If **NO DEAL**, continue by opening these four cases:

The bank offer is:

If **NO DEAL**, continue by opening these three cases:

The bank offer is:

If **NO DEAL**, continue by opening these two cases:

The bank offer is:

DEAL or **NO DEAL**

If **NO DEAL**, continue by opening this case:

The bank offer is:

DEAL or **NO DEAL**

If **NO DEAL**, continue by opening this case:

The bank offer is:

DEAL or **NO DEAL**

If **NO DEAL**, continue by opening this case:

The bank offer is:

DEAL or **NO DEAL**

If **NO DEAL**, continue by opening this case:

The bank offer is:

DEAL or **NO DEAL**

If **NO DEAL**, there are just two cases left. You can keep your original case or switch to the one at right. Choose one and open it.

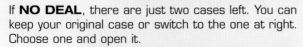

DEAL or **NO DEAL**

$		$	
$	.01	$	1,000
$	1	$	5,000
$	5	$	10,000
$	10	$	25,000
$	25	$	50,000
$	50	$	75,000
$	75	$	100,000
$	100	$	200,000
$	200	$	300,000
$	300	$	400,000
$	400	$	500,000
$	500	$	750,000
$	750	$	1,000,000

Here is your case: **DON'T OPEN IT!**

Start by opening these six cases:

The bank offer is:

DEAL NO DEAL

If **NO DEAL**, continue by opening these five cases:

The bank offer is:

DEAL NO DEAL

If **NO DEAL**, continue by opening these four cases:

The bank offer is:

DEAL NO DEAL

If **NO DEAL**, continue by opening these three cases:

The bank offer is:

DEAL NO DEAL

If **NO DEAL**, continue by opening these two cases:

The bank offer is: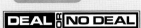

If **NO DEAL**, continue by opening this case:

The bank offer is:

If **NO DEAL**, continue by opening this case:

The bank offer is:

If **NO DEAL**, continue by opening this case:

The bank offer is: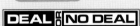

If **NO DEAL**, continue by opening this case:

The bank offer is: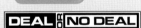

If **NO DEAL**, there are just two cases left. You can keep your original case or switch to the one at right. Choose one and open it.

DEAL or NO DEAL

$		$	
$	.01	$	1,000
$	1	$	5,000
$	5	$	10,000
$	10	$	25,000
$	25	$	50,000
$	50	$	75,000
$	75	$	100,000
$	100	$	200,000
$	200	$	300,000
$	300	$	400,000
$	400	$	500,000
$	500	$	750,000
$	750	$	1,000,000

Here is your case: **DON'T OPEN IT!**

Start by opening these six cases:

The bank offer is:

If **NO DEAL**, continue by opening these five cases:

The bank offer is:

If **NO DEAL**, continue by opening these four cases:

The bank offer is:

If **NO DEAL**, continue by opening these three cases:

The bank offer is:

If **NO DEAL**, continue by opening these two cases:

The bank offer is:

DEAL or **NO DEAL**

If **NO DEAL**, continue by opening this case:

The bank offer is: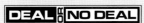

DEAL or **NO DEAL**

If **NO DEAL**, continue by opening this case:

The bank offer is: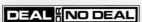

DEAL or **NO DEAL**

If **NO DEAL**, continue by opening this case:

The bank offer is: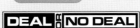

DEAL or **NO DEAL**

If **NO DEAL**, continue by opening this case:

The bank offer is: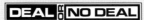

DEAL or **NO DEAL**

If **NO DEAL**, there are just two cases left. You can keep your original case or switch to the one at right. Choose one and open it.

DEAL or **NO DEAL**

$	.01	$ 1,000
$	1	$ 5,000
$	5	$ 10,000
$	10	$ 25,000
$	25	$ 50,000
$	50	$ 75,000
$	75	$ 100,000
$	100	$ 200,000
$	200	$ 300,000
$	300	$ 400,000
$	400	$ 500,000
$	500	$ 750,000
$	750	$ 1,000,000

Here is your case: **DON'T OPEN IT!**

Start by opening these six cases:

The bank offer is:

 **DEAL** or **NO DEAL**

If **NO DEAL**, continue by opening these five cases:

The bank offer is:

 **DEAL** or **NO DEAL**

If **NO DEAL**, continue by opening these four cases:

The bank offer is:

 **DEAL** or **NO DEAL**

If **NO DEAL**, continue by opening these three cases:

The bank offer is:

 **DEAL** or **NO DEAL**

If **NO DEAL**, continue by opening these two cases:

The bank offer is:

DEAL or **NO DEAL**

If **NO DEAL**, continue by opening this case:

The bank offer is:

DEAL or **NO DEAL**

If **NO DEAL**, continue by opening this case:

The bank offer is:

DEAL or **NO DEAL**

If **NO DEAL**, continue by opening this case:

The bank offer is:

DEAL or **NO DEAL**

If **NO DEAL**, continue by opening this case:

The bank offer is:

DEAL or **NO DEAL**

If **NO DEAL**, there are just two cases left. You can keep your original case or switch to the one at right. Choose one and open it.

DEAL or **NO DEAL**

$	.01	$	1,000
$	1	$	5,000
$	5	$	10,000
$	10	$	25,000
$	25	$	50,000
$	50	$	75,000
$	75	$	100,000
$	100	$	200,000
$	200	$	300,000
$	300	$	400,000
$	400	$	500,000
$	500	$	750,000
$	750	$	1,000,000

Here is your case: **DON'T OPEN IT!**

Start by opening these six cases:

The bank offer is:

If **NO DEAL**, continue by opening these five cases:

The bank offer is:

If **NO DEAL**, continue by opening these four cases:

The bank offer is:

If **NO DEAL**, continue by opening these three cases:

The bank offer is:

If **NO DEAL**, continue by opening these two cases:

The bank offer is:

DEAL or **NO DEAL**

If **NO DEAL**, continue by opening this case:

The bank offer is:

DEAL or **NO DEAL**

If **NO DEAL**, continue by opening this case:

The bank offer is:

DEAL or **NO DEAL**

If **NO DEAL**, continue by opening this case:

The bank offer is:

DEAL or **NO DEAL**

If **NO DEAL**, continue by opening this case:

The bank offer is:

DEAL or **NO DEAL**

If **NO DEAL**, there are just two cases left. You can keep your original case or switch to the one at right. Choose one and open it.

DEAL or **NO DEAL**

$		$	
$	.01	$	1,000
$	1	$	5,000
$	5	$	10,000
$	10	$	25,000
$	25	$	50,000
$	50	$	75,000
$	75	$	100,000
$	100	$	200,000
$	200	$	300,000
$	300	$	400,000
$	400	$	500,000
$	500	$	750,000
$	750	$	1,000,000

Here is your case: **DON'T OPEN IT!**

Start by opening these six cases:

The bank offer is:  DEAL OR NO DEAL

If **NO DEAL**, continue by opening these five cases:

The bank offer is:  DEAL OR NO DEAL

If **NO DEAL**, continue by opening these four cases:

The bank offer is:  DEAL OR NO DEAL

If **NO DEAL**, continue by opening these three cases:

The bank offer is:  DEAL OR NO DEAL

If **NO DEAL**, continue by opening these two cases:

The bank offer is:

DEAL or **NO DEAL**

If **NO DEAL**, continue by opening this case:

The bank offer is:

DEAL or **NO DEAL**

If **NO DEAL**, continue by opening this case:

The bank offer is:

DEAL or **NO DEAL**

If **NO DEAL**, continue by opening this case:

The bank offer is:

DEAL or **NO DEAL**

If **NO DEAL**, continue by opening this case:

The bank offer is:

DEAL or **NO DEAL**

If **NO DEAL**, there are just two cases left. You can keep your original case or switch to the one at right. Choose one and open it.

DEAL or **NO DEAL**

$		$	
$	.01	$	1,000
$	1	$	5,000
$	5	$	10,000
$	10	$	25,000
$	25	$	50,000
$	50	$	75,000
$	75	$	100,000
$	100	$	200,000
$	200	$	300,000
$	300	$	400,000
$	400	$	500,000
$	500	$	750,000
$	750	$	1,000,000

Here is your case: **DON'T OPEN IT!**

Start by opening these six cases:

The bank offer is: DEAL or NO DEAL

If **NO DEAL**, continue by opening these five cases:

The bank offer is: DEAL or NO DEAL

If **NO DEAL**, continue by opening these four cases:

The bank offer is: DEAL or NO DEAL

If **NO DEAL**, continue by opening these three cases:

The bank offer is: DEAL or NO DEAL

If **NO DEAL**, continue by opening these two cases:

The bank offer is:

DEAL or **NO DEAL**

If **NO DEAL**, continue by opening this case:

The bank offer is:

DEAL or **NO DEAL**

If **NO DEAL**, continue by opening this case:

The bank offer is:

DEAL or **NO DEAL**

If **NO DEAL**, continue by opening this case:

The bank offer is:

DEAL or **NO DEAL**

If **NO DEAL**, continue by opening this case:

The bank offer is:

DEAL or **NO DEAL**

If **NO DEAL**, there are just two cases left. You can keep your original case or switch to the one at right. Choose one and open it.

DEAL or **NO DEAL**

$		$	
$	.01	$	1,000
$	1	$	5,000
$	5	$	10,000
$	10	$	25,000
$	25	$	50,000
$	50	$	75,000
$	75	$	100,000
$	100	$	200,000
$	200	$	300,000
$	300	$	400,000
$	400	$	500,000
$	500	$	750,000
$	750	$	1,000,000

Here is your case: **DON'T OPEN IT!**

Start by opening these six cases:

The bank offer is:

If **NO DEAL**, continue by opening these five cases:

The bank offer is: **DEAL** or **NO DEAL**

If **NO DEAL**, continue by opening these four cases:

The bank offer is: **DEAL** or **NO DEAL**

If **NO DEAL**, continue by opening these three cases:

The bank offer is: **DEAL** or **NO DEAL**

If **NO DEAL**, continue by opening these two cases:

The bank offer is:

DEAL **NO DEAL**

If **NO DEAL**, continue by opening this case:

The bank offer is:

DEAL **NO DEAL**

If **NO DEAL**, continue by opening this case:

The bank offer is:

DEAL **NO DEAL**

If **NO DEAL**, continue by opening this case:

The bank offer is:

DEAL **NO DEAL**

If **NO DEAL**, continue by opening this case:

The bank offer is: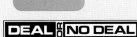

DEAL **NO DEAL**

If **NO DEAL**, there are just two cases left. You can keep your original case or switch to the one at right. Choose one and open it.

DEAL OR NO DEAL	
$ .01	$ 1,000
$ 1	$ 5,000
$ 5	$ 10,000
$ 10	$ 25,000
$ 25	$ 50,000
$ 50	$ 75,000
$ 75	$ 100,000
$ 100	$ 200,000
$ 200	$ 300,000
$ 300	$ 400,000
$ 400	$ 500,000
$ 500	$ 750,000
$ 750	$ 1,000,000

Here is your case: **DON'T OPEN IT!**

Start by opening these six cases:

The bank offer is:

If **NO DEAL**, continue by opening these five cases:

The bank offer is:

If **NO DEAL**, continue by opening these four cases:

The bank offer is:

If **NO DEAL**, continue by opening these three cases:

The bank offer is:

If **NO DEAL**, continue by opening these two cases:

The bank offer is:

DEAL or **NO DEAL**

If **NO DEAL**, continue by opening this case:

The bank offer is:

DEAL or **NO DEAL**

If **NO DEAL**, continue by opening this case:

The bank offer is:

DEAL or **NO DEAL**

If **NO DEAL**, continue by opening this case:

The bank offer is:

DEAL or **NO DEAL**

If **NO DEAL**, continue by opening this case:

The bank offer is:

DEAL or **NO DEAL**

If **NO DEAL**, there are just two cases left. You can keep your original case or switch to the one at right. Choose one and open it.

DEAL or **NO DEAL**

$	.01	$	1,000
$	1	$	5,000
$	5	$	10,000
$	10	$	25,000
$	25	$	50,000
$	50	$	75,000
$	75	$	100,000
$	100	$	200,000
$	200	$	300,000
$	300	$	400,000
$	400	$	500,000
$	500	$	750,000
$	750	$	1,000,000

Here is your case: **DON'T OPEN IT!**

Start by opening these six cases:

The bank offer is:  **DEAL ⅊ NO DEAL**

If **NO DEAL**, continue by opening these five cases:

The bank offer is: **DEAL ⅊ NO DEAL**

If **NO DEAL**, continue by opening these four cases:

The bank offer is:  **DEAL ⅊ NO DEAL**

If **NO DEAL**, continue by opening these three cases:

The bank offer is: **DEAL ⅊ NO DEAL**

If **NO DEAL**, continue by opening these two cases:

The bank offer is:

DEAL or **NO DEAL**

If **NO DEAL**, continue by opening this case:

The bank offer is: $160,0...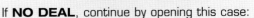

DEAL or **NO DEAL**

If **NO DEAL**, continue by opening this case:

The bank offer is:

DEAL or **NO DEAL**

If **NO DEAL**, continue by opening this case:

The bank offer is:

DEAL or **NO DEAL**

If **NO DEAL**, continue by opening this case:

The bank offer is:

DEAL or **NO DEAL**

If **NO DEAL**, there are just two cases left. You can keep your original case or switch to the one at right. Choose one and open it.

DEAL or NO DEAL

$	.01	$	1,000
$	1	$	5,000
$	5	$	10,000
$	10	$	25,000
$	25	$	50,000
$	50	$	75,000
$	75	$	100,000
$	100	$	200,000
$	200	$	300,000
$	300	$	400,000
$	400	$	500,000
$	500	$	750,000
$	750	$	1,000,000

Here is your case: **DON'T OPEN IT!**

Start by opening these six cases:

The bank offer is:  **DEAL** or **NO DEAL**

If **NO DEAL**, continue by opening these five cases:

The bank offer is:  **DEAL** or **NO DEAL**

If **NO DEAL**, continue by opening these four cases:

The bank offer is:  **DEAL** or **NO DEAL**

If **NO DEAL**, continue by opening these three cases:

The bank offer is:  **DEAL** or **NO DEAL**

If **NO DEAL**, continue by opening these two cases:

The bank offer is:

DEAL or **NO DEAL**

If **NO DEAL**, continue by opening this case:

The bank offer is:

DEAL or **NO DEAL**

If **NO DEAL**, continue by opening this case:

The bank offer is:

DEAL or **NO DEAL**

If **NO DEAL**, continue by opening this case:

The bank offer is:

DEAL or **NO DEAL**

If **NO DEAL**, continue by opening this case:

The bank offer is:

DEAL or **NO DEAL**

If **NO DEAL**, there are just two cases left. You can keep your original case or switch to the one at right. Choose one and open it.

DEAL or **NO DEAL**	
$ .01	$ 1,000
$ 1	$ 5,000
$ 5	$ 10,000
$ 10	$ 25,000
$ 25	$ 50,000
$ 50	$ 75,000
$ 75	$ 100,000
$ 100	$ 200,000
$ 200	$ 300,000
$ 300	$ 400,000
$ 400	$ 500,000
$ 500	$ 750,000
$ 750	$ 1,000,000

Here is your case: **DON'T OPEN IT!**

Start by opening these six cases:

The bank offer is:

 **DEAL** or **NO DEAL**

If **NO DEAL**, continue by opening these five cases:

The bank offer is:

 **DEAL** or **NO DEAL**

If **NO DEAL**, continue by opening these four cases:

The bank offer is:

 DEAL or **NO DEAL**

If **NO DEAL**, continue by opening these three cases:

The bank offer is:

 **DEAL** or **NO DEAL**

If **NO DEAL**, continue by opening these two cases:

The bank offer is:

DEAL or **NO DEAL**

If **NO DEAL**, continue by opening this case:

The bank offer is: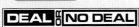

DEAL or **NO DEAL**

If **NO DEAL**, continue by opening this case:

The bank offer is:

DEAL or **NO DEAL**

If **NO DEAL**, continue by opening this case:

The bank offer is:

DEAL or **NO DEAL**

If **NO DEAL**, continue by opening this case:

The bank offer is:

DEAL or **NO DEAL**

If **NO DEAL**, there are just two cases left. You can keep your original case or switch to the one at right. Choose one and open it.

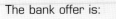

DEAL or NO DEAL

$		$	
$	.01	$	1,000
$	1	$	5,000
$	5	$	10,000
$	10	$	25,000
$	25	$	50,000
$	50	$	75,000
$	75	$	100,000
$	100	$	200,000
$	200	$	300,000
$	300	$	400,000
$	400	$	500,000
$	500	$	750,000
$	750	$	1,000,000

Here is your case: **DON'T OPEN IT!**

Start by opening these six cases:

The bank offer is:

If **NO DEAL**, continue by opening these five cases:

The bank offer is:

If **NO DEAL**, continue by opening these four cases:

The bank offer is:

If **NO DEAL**, continue by opening these three cases:

The bank offer is:

If **NO DEAL**, continue by opening these two cases:

The bank offer is:

DEAL or **NO DEAL**

If **NO DEAL**, continue by opening this case:

The bank offer is:

DEAL or **NO DEAL**

If **NO DEAL**, continue by opening this case:

The bank offer is:

DEAL or **NO DEAL**

If **NO DEAL**, continue by opening this case:

The bank offer is: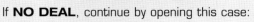

DEAL or **NO DEAL**

If **NO DEAL**, continue by opening this case:

The bank offer is:

DEAL or **NO DEAL**

If **NO DEAL**, there are just two cases left. You can keep your original case or switch to the one at right. Choose one and open it.

DEAL or **NO DEAL**

$		$	
$	.01	$	1,000
$	1	$	5,000
$	5	$	10,000
$	10	$	25,000
$	25	$	50,000
$	50	$	75,000
$	75	$	100,000
$	100	$	200,000
$	200	$	300,000
$	300	$	400,000
$	400	$	500,000
$	500	$	750,000
$	750	$	1,000,000

Here is your case: **DON'T OPEN IT!**

Start by opening these six cases:

The bank offer is:

If **NO DEAL**, continue by opening these five cases:

The bank offer is:

If **NO DEAL**, continue by opening these four cases:

The bank offer is:

If **NO DEAL**, continue by opening these three cases:

The bank offer is:

If **NO DEAL**, continue by opening these two cases:

The bank offer is: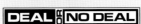

DEAL or **NO DEAL**

If **NO DEAL**, continue by opening this case:

The bank offer is:

DEAL or **NO DEAL**

If **NO DEAL**, continue by opening this case:

The bank offer is:

DEAL or **NO DEAL**

If **NO DEAL**, continue by opening this case:

The bank offer is: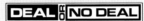

DEAL or **NO DEAL**

If **NO DEAL**, continue by opening this case:

The bank offer is:

DEAL or **NO DEAL**

If **NO DEAL**, there are just two cases left. You can keep your original case or switch to the one at right. Choose one and open it.

DEAL or NO DEAL	
$ .01	$ 1,000
$ 1	$ 5,000
$ 5	$ 10,000
$ 10	$ 25,000
$ 25	$ 50,000
$ 50	$ 75,000
$ 75	$ 100,000
$ 100	$ 200,000
$ 200	$ 300,000
$ 300	$ 400,000
$ 400	$ 500,000
$ 500	$ 750,000
$ 750	$ 1,000,000

Here is your case: **DON'T OPEN IT!**

Start by opening these six cases:

The bank offer is:  **DEAL or NO DEAL**

If **NO DEAL**, continue by opening these five cases:

The bank offer is:  **DEAL or NO DEAL**

If **NO DEAL**, continue by opening these four cases:

The bank offer is:  **DEAL or NO DEAL**

If **NO DEAL**, continue by opening these three cases:

The bank offer is:  **DEAL or NO DEAL**

If **NO DEAL**, continue by opening these two cases:

The bank offer is:

If **NO DEAL**, continue by opening this case:

The bank offer is:

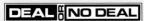

If **NO DEAL**, continue by opening this case:

The bank offer is:

DEAL or NO DEAL

If **NO DEAL**, continue by opening this case:

The bank offer is:

DEAL or NO DEAL

If **NO DEAL**, continue by opening this case:

The bank offer is:

DEAL or NO DEAL

If **NO DEAL**, there are just two cases left. You can keep your original case or switch to the one at right. Choose one and open it.

DEAL or NO DEAL

$		$	
$	.01	$	1,000
$	1	$	5,000
$	5	$	10,000
$	10	$	25,000
$	25	$	50,000
$	50	$	75,000
$	75	$	100,000
$	100	$	200,000
$	200	$	300,000
$	300	$	400,000
$	400	$	500,000
$	500	$	750,000
$	750	$	1,000,000

Here is your case: **DON'T OPEN IT!**

Start by opening these six cases:

The bank offer is:  **DEAL** or **NO DEAL**

If **NO DEAL**, continue by opening these five cases:

The bank offer is:  **DEAL** or **NO DEAL**

If **NO DEAL**, continue by opening these four cases:

The bank offer is:  **DEAL** or **NO DEAL**

If **NO DEAL**, continue by opening these three cases:

The bank offer is:  **DEAL** or **NO DEAL**

If **NO DEAL**, continue by opening these two cases:

The bank offer is: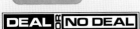

DEAL or **NO DEAL**

If **NO DEAL**, continue by opening this case:

The bank offer is: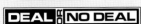

DEAL or **NO DEAL**

If **NO DEAL**, continue by opening this case:

The bank offer is:

DEAL or **NO DEAL**

If **NO DEAL**, continue by opening this case:

The bank offer is:

DEAL or **NO DEAL**

If **NO DEAL**, continue by opening this case:

The bank offer is: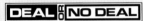

DEAL or **NO DEAL**

If **NO DEAL**, there are just two cases left. You can keep your original case or switch to the one at right. Choose one and open it.

DEAL or NO DEAL	
$ .01	$ 1,000
$ 1	$ 5,000
$ 5	$ 10,000
$ 10	$ 25,000
$ 25	$ 50,000
$ 50	$ 75,000
$ 75	$ 100,000
$ 100	$ 200,000
$ 200	$ 300,000
$ 300	$ 400,000
$ 400	$ 500,000
$ 500	$ 750,000
$ 750	$ 1,000,000

Here is your case: **DON'T OPEN IT!**

Start by opening these six cases:

The bank offer is:

If **NO DEAL**, continue by opening these five cases:

The bank offer is:

If **NO DEAL**, continue by opening these four cases:

The bank offer is:

If **NO DEAL**, continue by opening these three cases:

The bank offer is:

If **NO DEAL**, continue by opening these two cases:

The bank offer is: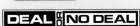

DEAL or **NO DEAL**

If **NO DEAL**, continue by opening this case:

The bank offer is:

DEAL or **NO DEAL**

If **NO DEAL**, continue by opening this case:

The bank offer is: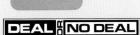

DEAL or **NO DEAL**

If **NO DEAL**, continue by opening this case:

The bank offer is:

DEAL or **NO DEAL**

If **NO DEAL**, continue by opening this case:

The bank offer is:

DEAL or **NO DEAL**

If **NO DEAL**, there are just two cases left. You can keep your original case or switch to the one at right. Choose one and open it.

DEAL or **NO DEAL**	
$ .01	$ 1,000
$ 1	$ 5,000
$ 5	$ 10,000
$ 10	$ 25,000
$ 25	$ 50,000
$ 50	$ 75,000
$ 75	$ 100,000
$ 100	$ 200,000
$ 200	$ 300,000
$ 300	$ 400,000
$ 400	$ 500,000
$ 500	$ 750,000
$ 750	$ 1,000,000

Here is your case: **DON'T OPEN IT!**

Start by opening these six cases:

The bank offer is:

DEAL or NO DEAL

If **NO DEAL**, continue by opening these five cases:

The bank offer is:

DEAL or NO DEAL

If **NO DEAL**, continue by opening these four cases:

The bank offer is:

DEAL or NO DEAL

If **NO DEAL**, continue by opening these three cases:

The bank offer is:

DEAL or NO DEAL

If **NO DEAL**, continue by opening these two cases:

The bank offer is:

DEAL or NO DEAL

If **NO DEAL**, continue by opening this case:

The bank offer is: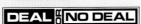

DEAL or NO DEAL

If **NO DEAL**, continue by opening this case:

The bank offer is: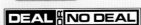

DEAL or NO DEAL

If **NO DEAL**, continue by opening this case:

The bank offer is:

DEAL or NO DEAL

If **NO DEAL**, continue by opening this case:

The bank offer is:

DEAL or NO DEAL

If **NO DEAL**, there are just two cases left. You can keep your original case or switch to the one at right. Choose one and open it.

DEAL or NO DEAL

$		$	
$	.01	$	1,000
$	1	$	5,000
$	5	$	10,000
$	10	$	25,000
$	25	$	50,000
$	50	$	75,000
$	75	$	100,000
$	100	$	200,000
$	200	$	300,000
$	300	$	400,000
$	400	$	500,000
$	500	$	750,000
$	750	$	1,000,000

Here is your case: **DON'T OPEN IT!**

Start by opening these six cases:

The bank offer is: **DEAL ⸮ NO DEAL**

If **NO DEAL**, continue by opening these five cases:

The bank offer is: **DEAL ⸮ NO DEAL**

If **NO DEAL**, continue by opening these four cases:

The bank offer is: **DEAL ⸮ NO DEAL**

If **NO DEAL**, continue by opening these three cases:

The bank offer is: **DEAL ⸮ NO DEAL**

If **NO DEAL**, continue by opening these two cases:

The bank offer is:

If **NO DEAL**, continue by opening this case:

The bank offer is:

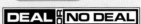

If **NO DEAL**, continue by opening this case:

The bank offer is:

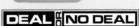

If **NO DEAL**, continue by opening this case:

The bank offer is:

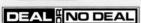

If **NO DEAL**, continue by opening this case:

The bank offer is:

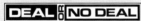

If **NO DEAL**, there are just two cases left. You can keep your original case or switch to the one at right. Choose one and open it.

DEAL or NO DEAL	
$ .01	$ 1,000
$ 1	$ 5,000
$ 5	$ 10,000
$ 10	$ 25,000
$ 25	$ 50,000
$ 50	$ 75,000
$ 75	$ 100,000
$ 100	$ 200,000
$ 200	$ 300,000
$ 300	$ 400,000
$ 400	$ 500,000
$ 500	$ 750,000
$ 750	$ 1,000,000

Here is your case: **DON'T OPEN IT!**

Start by opening these six cases:

The bank offer is:

If **NO DEAL**, continue by opening these five cases:

The bank offer is:

If **NO DEAL**, continue by opening these four cases:

The bank offer is:

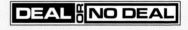

If **NO DEAL**, continue by opening these three cases:

The bank offer is:

If **NO DEAL**, continue by opening these two cases:

The bank offer is:

DEAL or **NO DEAL**

If **NO DEAL**, continue by opening this case:

The bank offer is: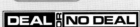

DEAL or **NO DEAL**

If **NO DEAL**, continue by opening this case:

The bank offer is: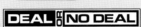

DEAL or **NO DEAL**

If **NO DEAL**, continue by opening this case:

The bank offer is:

DEAL or **NO DEAL**

If **NO DEAL**, continue by opening this case:

The bank offer is:

DEAL or **NO DEAL**

If **NO DEAL**, there are just two cases left. You can keep your original case or switch to the one at right. Choose one and open it.

DEAL or NO DEAL

$ .01	$ 1,000
$ 1	$ 5,000
$ 5	$ 10,000
$ 10	$ 25,000
$ 25	$ 50,000
$ 50	$ 75,000
$ 75	$ 100,000
$ 100	$ 200,000
$ 200	$ 300,000
$ 300	$ 400,000
$ 400	$ 500,000
$ 500	$ 750,000
$ 750	$ 1,000,000

Here is your case: **DON'T OPEN IT!**

Start by opening these six cases:

The bank offer is:  **DEAL** or **NO DEAL**

If **NO DEAL**, continue by opening these five cases:

The bank offer is:  **DEAL** or **NO DEAL**

If **NO DEAL**, continue by opening these four cases:

The bank offer is:  **DEAL** or **NO DEAL**

If **NO DEAL**, continue by opening these three cases:

The bank offer is:  **DEAL** or **NO DEAL**

If **NO DEAL**, continue by opening these two cases:

The bank offer is:

DEAL or **NO DEAL**

If **NO DEAL**, continue by opening this case:

The bank offer is:

DEAL or **NO DEAL**

If **NO DEAL**, continue by opening this case:

The bank offer is:

DEAL or **NO DEAL**

If **NO DEAL**, continue by opening this case:

The bank offer is:

DEAL or **NO DEAL**

If **NO DEAL**, continue by opening this case:

The bank offer is:

DEAL or **NO DEAL**

If **NO DEAL**, there are just two cases left. You can keep your original case or switch to the one at right. Choose one and open it.

DEAL or **NO DEAL**	
$ .01	$ 1,000
$ 1	$ 5,000
$ 5	$ 10,000
$ 10	$ 25,000
$ 25	$ 50,000
$ 50	$ 75,000
$ 75	$ 100,000
$ 100	$ 200,000
$ 200	$ 300,000
$ 300	$ 400,000
$ 400	$ 500,000
$ 500	$ 750,000
$ 750	$ 1,000,000

Here is your case: **DON'T OPEN IT!**

Start by opening these six cases:

The bank offer is:  **DEAL** or **NO DEAL**

If **NO DEAL**, continue by opening these five cases:

The bank offer is:  **DEAL** or **NO DEAL**

If **NO DEAL**, continue by opening these four cases:

The bank offer is:  **DEAL** or **NO DEAL**

If **NO DEAL**, continue by opening these three cases:

The bank offer is:  **DEAL** or **NO DEAL**

If **NO DEAL**, continue by opening these two cases:

The bank offer is: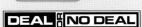

DEAL or **NO DEAL**

If **NO DEAL**, continue by opening this case:

The bank offer is:

DEAL or **NO DEAL**

If **NO DEAL**, continue by opening this case:

The bank offer is:

DEAL or **NO DEAL**

If **NO DEAL**, continue by opening this case:

The bank offer is:

DEAL or **NO DEAL**

If **NO DEAL**, continue by opening this case:

The bank offer is: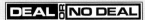

DEAL or **NO DEAL**

If **NO DEAL**, there are just two cases left. You can keep your original case or switch to the one at right. Choose one and open it.

DEAL or **NO DEAL**	
$ .01	$ 1,000
$ 1	$ 5,000
$ 5	$ 10,000
$ 10	$ 25,000
$ 25	$ 50,000
$ 50	$ 75,000
$ 75	$ 100,000
$ 100	$ 200,000
$ 200	$ 300,000
$ 300	$ 400,000
$ 400	$ 500,000
$ 500	$ 750,000
$ 750	$ 1,000,000

Here is your case: **DON'T OPEN IT!**

Start by opening these six cases:

The bank offer is:

 DEAL OR NO DEAL

If **NO DEAL**, continue by opening these five cases:

The bank offer is:

 DEAL OR NO DEAL

If **NO DEAL**, continue by opening these four cases:

The bank offer is:

 DEAL OR NO DEAL

If **NO DEAL**, continue by opening these three cases:

The bank offer is:

 DEAL OR NO DEAL

If **NO DEAL**, continue by opening these two cases:

The bank offer is: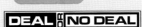

DEAL or **NO DEAL**

If **NO DEAL**, continue by opening this case:

The bank offer is: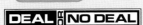

DEAL or **NO DEAL**

If **NO DEAL**, continue by opening this case:

The bank offer is: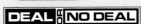

DEAL or **NO DEAL**

If **NO DEAL**, continue by opening this case:

The bank offer is: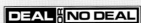

DEAL or **NO DEAL**

If **NO DEAL**, continue by opening this case:

The bank offer is: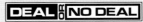

DEAL or **NO DEAL**

If **NO DEAL**, there are just two cases left. You can keep your original case or switch to the one at right. Choose one and open it.

DEAL or **NO DEAL**

$		$	
$	.01	$	1,000
$	1	$	5,000
$	5	$	10,000
$	10	$	25,000
$	25	$	50,000
$	50	$	75,000
$	75	$	100,000
$	100	$	200,000
$	200	$	300,000
$	300	$	400,000
$	400	$	500,000
$	500	$	750,000
$	750	$	1,000,000

Here is your case: **DON'T OPEN IT!**

Start by opening these six cases:

The bank offer is:

If **NO DEAL**, continue by opening these five cases:

The bank offer is:

If **NO DEAL**, continue by opening these four cases:

The bank offer is:

If **NO DEAL**, continue by opening these three cases:

The bank offer is:

If **NO DEAL**, continue by opening these two cases:

The bank offer is: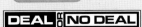

DEAL or **NO DEAL**

If **NO DEAL**, continue by opening this case:

The bank offer is: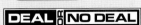

DEAL or **NO DEAL**

If **NO DEAL**, continue by opening this case:

The bank offer is: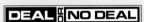

DEAL or **NO DEAL**

If **NO DEAL**, continue by opening this case:

The bank offer is:

DEAL or **NO DEAL**

If **NO DEAL**, continue by opening this case:

The bank offer is:

DEAL or **NO DEAL**

If **NO DEAL**, there are just two cases left. You can keep your original case or switch to the one at right. Choose one and open it.

DEAL or **NO DEAL**

$ .01	$ 1,000
$ 1	$ 5,000
$ 5	$ 10,000
$ 10	$ 25,000
$ 25	$ 50,000
$ 50	$ 75,000
$ 75	$ 100,000
$ 100	$ 200,000
$ 200	$ 300,000
$ 300	$ 400,000
$ 400	$ 500,000
$ 500	$ 750,000
$ 750	$ 1,000,000

Here is your case: **DON'T OPEN IT!**

Start by opening these six cases:

The bank offer is:  DEAL or NO DEAL

If **NO DEAL**, continue by opening these five cases:

The bank offer is:  DEAL or NO DEAL

If **NO DEAL**, continue by opening these four cases:

The bank offer is:  DEAL or NO DEAL

If **NO DEAL**, continue by opening these three cases:

The bank offer is:  DEAL or NO DEAL

If **NO DEAL**, continue by opening these two cases:

The bank offer is:

DEAL or **NO DEAL**

If **NO DEAL**, continue by opening this case:

The bank offer is: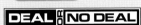

DEAL or **NO DEAL**

If **NO DEAL**, continue by opening this case:

The bank offer is: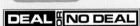

DEAL or **NO DEAL**

If **NO DEAL**, continue by opening this case:

The bank offer is:

DEAL or **NO DEAL**

If **NO DEAL**, continue by opening this case:

The bank offer is:

DEAL or **NO DEAL**

If **NO DEAL**, there are just two cases left. You can keep your original case or switch to the one at right. Choose one and open it.

DEAL or **NO DEAL**	
$ .01	$ 1,000
$ 1	$ 5,000
$ 5	$ 10,000
$ 10	$ 25,000
$ 25	$ 50,000
$ 50	$ 75,000
$ 75	$ 100,000
$ 100	$ 200,000
$ 200	$ 300,000
$ 300	$ 400,000
$ 400	$ 500,000
$ 500	$ 750,000
$ 750	$ 1,000,000

Here is your case: **DON'T OPEN IT!**

Start by opening these six cases:

The bank offer is:

If **NO DEAL**, continue by opening these five cases:

The bank offer is:

If **NO DEAL**, continue by opening these four cases:

The bank offer is:

If **NO DEAL**, continue by opening these three cases:

The bank offer is:

If **NO DEAL**, continue by opening these two cases:

The bank offer is: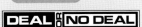

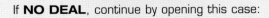

If **NO DEAL**, continue by opening this case:

The bank offer is: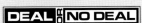

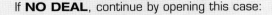

If **NO DEAL**, continue by opening this case:

The bank offer is:

If **NO DEAL**, continue by opening this case:

The bank offer is:

If **NO DEAL**, continue by opening this case:

The bank offer is:

If **NO DEAL**, there are just two cases left. You can keep your original case or switch to the one at right. Choose one and open it.

DEAL or NO DEAL	
$ .01	$ 1,000
$ 1	$ 5,000
$ 5	$ 10,000
$ 10	$ 25,000
$ 25	$ 50,000
$ 50	$ 75,000
$ 75	$ 100,000
$ 100	$ 200,000
$ 200	$ 300,000
$ 300	$ 400,000
$ 400	$ 500,000
$ 500	$ 750,000
$ 750	$ 1,000,000

Here is your case: **DON'T OPEN IT!**

Start by opening these six cases:

The bank offer is:

If **NO DEAL**, continue by opening these five cases:

The bank offer is:

If **NO DEAL**, continue by opening these four cases:

The bank offer is:

If **NO DEAL**, continue by opening these three cases:

The bank offer is:

If **NO DEAL**, continue by opening these two cases:

The bank offer is:

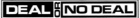

If **NO DEAL**, continue by opening this case:

The bank offer is:

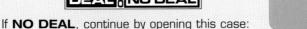

If **NO DEAL**, continue by opening this case:

The bank offer is:

DEAL or NO DEAL

If **NO DEAL**, continue by opening this case:

The bank offer is:

DEAL or NO DEAL

If **NO DEAL**, continue by opening this case:

The bank offer is:

DEAL or NO DEAL

If **NO DEAL**, there are just two cases left. You can keep your original case or switch to the one at right. Choose one and open it.

DEAL or	NO DEAL
$ .01	$ 1,000
$ 1	$ 5,000
$ 5	$ 10,000
$ 10	$ 25,000
$ 25	$ 50,000
$ 50	$ 75,000
$ 75	$ 100,000
$ 100	$ 200,000
$ 200	$ 300,000
$ 300	$ 400,000
$ 400	$ 500,000
$ 500	$ 750,000
$ 750	$ 1,000,000

Here is your case: **DON'T OPEN IT!**

Start by opening these six cases:

The bank offer is:

If **NO DEAL**, continue by opening these five cases:

The bank offer is:

If **NO DEAL**, continue by opening these four cases:

The bank offer is:

If **NO DEAL**, continue by opening these three cases:

The bank offer is:

If **NO DEAL**, continue by opening these two cases:

The bank offer is:

DEAL or **NO DEAL**

If **NO DEAL**, continue by opening this case:

The bank offer is: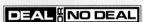

DEAL or **NO DEAL**

If **NO DEAL**, continue by opening this case:

The bank offer is: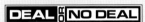

DEAL or **NO DEAL**

If **NO DEAL**, continue by opening this case:

The bank offer is:

DEAL or **NO DEAL**

If **NO DEAL**, continue by opening this case:

The bank offer is:

DEAL or **NO DEAL**

If **NO DEAL**, there are just two cases left. You can keep your original case or switch to the one at right. Choose one and open it.

DEAL or NO DEAL

$ .01	$ 1,000
$ 1	$ 5,000
$ 5	$ 10,000
$ 10	$ 25,000
$ 25	$ 50,000
$ 50	$ 75,000
$ 75	$ 100,000
$ 100	$ 200,000
$ 200	$ 300,000
$ 300	$ 400,000
$ 400	$ 500,000
$ 500	$ 750,000
$ 750	$ 1,000,000

Here is your case: **DON'T OPEN IT!**

Start by opening these six cases:

The bank offer is:

If **NO DEAL**, continue by opening these five cases:

The bank offer is:

If **NO DEAL**, continue by opening these four cases:

The bank offer is:

If **NO DEAL**, continue by opening these three cases:

The bank offer is:

If **NO DEAL**, continue by opening these two cases:

The bank offer is:

If **NO DEAL**, continue by opening this case:

The bank offer is:

DEAL **OR** NO DEAL

If **NO DEAL**, continue by opening this case:

The bank offer is:

DEAL **OR** NO DEAL

If **NO DEAL**, continue by opening this case:

The bank offer is:

DEAL **OR** NO DEAL

If **NO DEAL**, continue by opening this case:

The bank offer is:

DEAL **OR** NO DEAL

If **NO DEAL**, there are just two cases left. You can keep your original case or switch to the one at right. Choose one and open it.

DEAL **OR** NO DEAL	
$ .01	$ 1,000
$ 1	$ 5,000
$ 5	$ 10,000
$ 10	$ 25,000
$ 25	$ 50,000
$ 50	$ 75,000
$ 75	$ 100,000
$ 100	$ 200,000
$ 200	$ 300,000
$ 300	$ 400,000
$ 400	$ 500,000
$ 500	$ 750,000
$ 750	$ 1,000,000

Here is your case: **DON'T OPEN IT!**

Start by opening these six cases:

The bank offer is:

If **NO DEAL**, continue by opening these five cases:

The bank offer is:

If **NO DEAL**, continue by opening these four cases:

The bank offer is:

If **NO DEAL**, continue by opening these three cases:

The bank offer is:

If **NO DEAL**, continue by opening these two cases:

The bank offer is: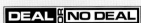

DEAL or NO DEAL

If **NO DEAL**, continue by opening this case:

The bank offer is: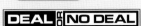

DEAL or NO DEAL

If **NO DEAL**, continue by opening this case:

The bank offer is:

DEAL or NO DEAL

If **NO DEAL**, continue by opening this case:

The bank offer is:

DEAL or NO DEAL

If **NO DEAL**, continue by opening this case:

The bank offer is:

DEAL or NO DEAL

If **NO DEAL**, there are just two cases left. You can keep your original case or switch to the one at right. Choose one and open it.

DEAL or NO DEAL	
$ .01	$ 1,000
$ 1	$ 5,000
$ 5	$ 10,000
$ 10	$ 25,000
$ 25	$ 50,000
$ 50	$ 75,000
$ 75	$ 100,000
$ 100	$ 200,000
$ 200	$ 300,000
$ 300	$ 400,000
$ 400	$ 500,000
$ 500	$ 750,000
$ 750	$ 1,000,000

Here is your case: **DON'T OPEN IT!**

Start by opening these six cases:

The bank offer is:

If **NO DEAL**, continue by opening these five cases:

The bank offer is:

If **NO DEAL**, continue by opening these four cases:

The bank offer is:

If **NO DEAL**, continue by opening these three cases:

The bank offer is:

If **NO DEAL**, continue by opening these two cases:

The bank offer is:

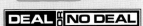

DEAL OR **NO DEAL**

If **NO DEAL**, continue by opening this case:

The bank offer is: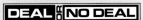

DEAL OR **NO DEAL**

If **NO DEAL**, continue by opening this case:

The bank offer is: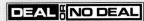

DEAL OR **NO DEAL**

If **NO DEAL**, continue by opening this case:

The bank offer is:

DEAL OR **NO DEAL**

If **NO DEAL**, continue by opening this case:

The bank offer is:

DEAL OR **NO DEAL**

If **NO DEAL**, there are just two cases left. You can keep your original case or switch to the one at right. Choose one and open it.

DEAL OR **NO DEAL**

$	.01	$	1,000
$	1	$	5,000
$	5	$	10,000
$	10	$	25,000
$	25	$	50,000
$	50	$	75,000
$	75	$	100,000
$	100	$	200,000
$	200	$	300,000
$	300	$	400,000
$	400	$	500,000
$	500	$	750,000
$	750	$	1,000,000

Here is your case: **DON'T OPEN IT!**

Start by opening these six cases:

The bank offer is:

If **NO DEAL**, continue by opening these five cases:

The bank offer is:

If **NO DEAL**, continue by opening these four cases:

The bank offer is:

If **NO DEAL**, continue by opening these three cases:

The bank offer is:

If **NO DEAL**, continue by opening these two cases:

The bank offer is: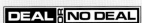

DEAL or NO DEAL

If **NO DEAL**, continue by opening this case:

The bank offer is:

DEAL or NO DEAL

If **NO DEAL**, continue by opening this case:

The bank offer is:

DEAL or NO DEAL

If **NO DEAL**, continue by opening this case:

The bank offer is:

DEAL or NO DEAL

If **NO DEAL**, continue by opening this case:

The bank offer is:

DEAL or NO DEAL

If **NO DEAL**, there are just two cases left. You can keep your original case or switch to the one at right. Choose one and open it.

DEAL or NO DEAL

$		$	
$	.01	$	1,000
$	1	$	5,000
$	5	$	10,000
$	10	$	25,000
$	25	$	50,000
$	50	$	75,000
$	75	$	100,000
$	100	$	200,000
$	200	$	300,000
$	300	$	400,000
$	400	$	500,000
$	500	$	750,000
$	750	$	1,000,000

Here is your case: **DON'T OPEN IT!**

Start by opening these six cases:

The bank offer is:
 **DEAL** or **NO DEAL**

If **NO DEAL**, continue by opening these five cases:

The bank offer is:
 **DEAL** or **NO DEAL**

If **NO DEAL**, continue by opening these four cases:

The bank offer is:
 **DEAL** or **NO DEAL**

If **NO DEAL**, continue by opening these three cases:

The bank offer is:
 **DEAL** or **NO DEAL**

If **NO DEAL**, continue by opening these two cases:

The bank offer is:

DEAL or **NO DEAL**

If **NO DEAL**, continue by opening this case:

The bank offer is:

DEAL or **NO DEAL**

If **NO DEAL**, continue by opening this case:

The bank offer is:

DEAL or **NO DEAL**

If **NO DEAL**, continue by opening this case:

The bank offer is:

DEAL or **NO DEAL**

If **NO DEAL**, continue by opening this case:

The bank offer is:

DEAL or **NO DEAL**

If **NO DEAL**, there are just two cases left. You can keep your original case or switch to the one at right. Choose one and open it.

DEAL or **NO DEAL**	
$ .01	$ 1,000
$ 1	$ 5,000
$ 5	$ 10,000
$ 10	$ 25,000
$ 25	$ 50,000
$ 50	$ 75,000
$ 75	$ 100,000
$ 100	$ 200,000
$ 200	$ 300,000
$ 300	$ 400,000
$ 400	$ 500,000
$ 500	$ 750,000
$ 750	$ 1,000,000

Here is your case: **DON'T OPEN IT!**

Start by opening these six cases:

The bank offer is:  **DEAL** or **NO DEAL**

If **NO DEAL**, continue by opening these five cases:

The bank offer is:  **DEAL** or **NO DEAL**

If **NO DEAL**, continue by opening these four cases:

The bank offer is:  **DEAL** or **NO DEAL**

If **NO DEAL**, continue by opening these three cases:

The bank offer is:  **DEAL** or **NO DEAL**

If **NO DEAL**, continue by opening these two cases:

The bank offer is:

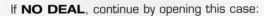

If **NO DEAL**, continue by opening this case:

The bank offer is:

If **NO DEAL**, continue by opening this case:

The bank offer is: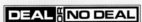

If **NO DEAL**, continue by opening this case:

The bank offer is:

If **NO DEAL**, continue by opening this case:

The bank offer is:

If **NO DEAL**, there are just two cases left. You can keep your original case or switch to the one at right. Choose one and open it.

DEAL or NO DEAL

$	.01	$	1,000
$	1	$	5,000
$	5	$	10,000
$	10	$	25,000
$	25	$	50,000
$	50	$	75,000
$	75	$	100,000
$	100	$	200,000
$	200	$	300,000
$	300	$	400,000
$	400	$	500,000
$	500	$	750,000
$	750	$	1,000,000

Here is your case: **DON'T OPEN IT!**

Start by opening these six cases:

The bank offer is:

If **NO DEAL**, continue by opening these five cases:

The bank offer is:

If **NO DEAL**, continue by opening these four cases:

The bank offer is:

If **NO DEAL**, continue by opening these three cases:

The bank offer is:

If **NO DEAL**, continue by opening these two cases:

The bank offer is: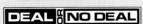

DEAL or **NO DEAL**

If **NO DEAL**, continue by opening this case:

The bank offer is: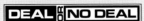

DEAL or **NO DEAL**

If **NO DEAL**, continue by opening this case:

The bank offer is: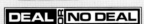

DEAL or **NO DEAL**

If **NO DEAL**, continue by opening this case:

The bank offer is:

DEAL or **NO DEAL**

If **NO DEAL**, continue by opening this case:

The bank offer is:

DEAL or **NO DEAL**

If **NO DEAL**, there are just two cases left. You can keep your original case or switch to the one at right. Choose one and open it.

DEAL or **NO DEAL**

$	.01	$	1,000
$	1	$	5,000
$	5	$	10,000
$	10	$	25,000
$	25	$	50,000
$	50	$	75,000
$	75	$	100,000
$	100	$	200,000
$	200	$	300,000
$	300	$	400,000
$	400	$	500,000
$	500	$	750,000
$	750	$	1,000,000

Here is your case: **DON'T OPEN IT!**

Start by opening these six cases:

The bank offer is: **DEAL** or **NO DEAL**

If **NO DEAL**, continue by opening these five cases:

The bank offer is: **DEAL** or **NO DEAL**

If **NO DEAL**, continue by opening these four cases:

The bank offer is: **DEAL** or **NO DEAL**

If **NO DEAL**, continue by opening these three cases:

The bank offer is: **DEAL** or **NO DEAL**

If **NO DEAL**, continue by opening these two cases:

The bank offer is:

If **NO DEAL**, continue by opening this case:

The bank offer is:

If **NO DEAL**, continue by opening this case:

The bank offer is:

If **NO DEAL**, continue by opening this case:

The bank offer is:

If **NO DEAL**, continue by opening this case:

The bank offer is:

If **NO DEAL**, there are just two cases left. You can keep your original case or switch to the one at right. Choose one and open it.

DEAL ȣ NO DEAL	
$ .01	$ 1,000
$ 1	$ 5,000
$ 5	$ 10,000
$ 10	$ 25,000
$ 25	$ 50,000
$ 50	$ 75,000
$ 75	$ 100,000
$ 100	$ 200,000
$ 200	$ 300,000
$ 300	$ 400,000
$ 400	$ 500,000
$ 500	$ 750,000
$ 750	$ 1,000,000

Here is your case: **DON'T OPEN IT!**

Start by opening these six cases:

The bank offer is:

If **NO DEAL**, continue by opening these five cases:

The bank offer is:

If **NO DEAL**, continue by opening these four cases:

The bank offer is:

If **NO DEAL**, continue by opening these three cases:

The bank offer is: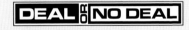

If **NO DEAL**, continue by opening these two cases:

The bank offer is:

If **NO DEAL**, continue by opening this case:

The bank offer is:

If **NO DEAL**, continue by opening this case:

The bank offer is:

If **NO DEAL**, continue by opening this case:

The bank offer is:

If **NO DEAL**, continue by opening this case:

The bank offer is:

If **NO DEAL**, there are just two cases left. You can keep your original case or switch to the one at right. Choose one and open it.

DEAL or NO DEAL	
$ .01	$ 1,000
$ 1	$ 5,000
$ 5	$ 10,000
$ 10	$ 25,000
$ 25	$ 50,000
$ 50	$ 75,000
$ 75	$ 100,000
$ 100	$ 200,000
$ 200	$ 300,000
$ 300	$ 400,000
$ 400	$ 500,000
$ 500	$ 750,000
$ 750	$ 1,000,000

Here is your case: **DON'T OPEN IT!**

Start by opening these six cases:

The bank offer is:

If **NO DEAL**, continue by opening these five cases:

The bank offer is:

If **NO DEAL**, continue by opening these four cases:

The bank offer is:

If **NO DEAL**, continue by opening these three cases:

The bank offer is:

If **NO DEAL**, continue by opening these two cases:

The bank offer is: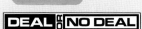

DEAL or **NO DEAL**

If **NO DEAL**, continue by opening this case:

The bank offer is:

DEAL or **NO DEAL**

If **NO DEAL**, continue by opening this case:

The bank offer is: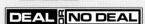

DEAL or **NO DEAL**

If **NO DEAL**, continue by opening this case:

The bank offer is:

DEAL or **NO DEAL**

If **NO DEAL**, continue by opening this case:

The bank offer is:

DEAL or **NO DEAL**

If **NO DEAL**, there are just two cases left. You can keep your original case or switch to the one at right. Choose one and open it.

DEAL or **NO DEAL**

$ .01	$ 1,000
$ 1	$ 5,000
$ 5	$ 10,000
$ 10	$ 25,000
$ 25	$ 50,000
$ 50	$ 75,000
$ 75	$ 100,000
$ 100	$ 200,000
$ 200	$ 300,000
$ 300	$ 400,000
$ 400	$ 500,000
$ 500	$ 750,000
$ 750	$ 1,000,000

Here is your case: **DON'T OPEN IT!**

Start by opening these six cases:

The bank offer is:  **DEAL or NO DEAL**

If **NO DEAL**, continue by opening these five cases:

The bank offer is:  **DEAL or NO DEAL**

If **NO DEAL**, continue by opening these four cases:

The bank offer is:  **DEAL or NO DEAL**

If **NO DEAL**, continue by opening these three cases:

The bank offer is:  **DEAL or NO DEAL**

If **NO DEAL**, continue by opening these two cases:

The bank offer is:

DEAL or **NO DEAL**

If **NO DEAL**, continue by opening this case:

The bank offer is:

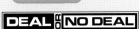

DEAL or **NO DEAL**

If **NO DEAL**, continue by opening this case:

The bank offer is:

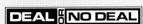

DEAL or **NO DEAL**

If **NO DEAL**, continue by opening this case:

The bank offer is:

DEAL or **NO DEAL**

If **NO DEAL**, continue by opening this case:

The bank offer is:

DEAL or **NO DEAL**

If **NO DEAL**, there are just two cases left. You can keep your original case or switch to the one at right. Choose one and open it.

DEAL or **NO DEAL**	
$ .01	$ 1,000
$ 1	$ 5,000
$ 5	$ 10,000
$ 10	$ 25,000
$ 25	$ 50,000
$ 50	$ 75,000
$ 75	$ 100,000
$ 100	$ 200,000
$ 200	$ 300,000
$ 300	$ 400,000
$ 400	$ 500,000
$ 500	$ 750,000
$ 750	$ 1,000,000

Here is your case: **DON'T OPEN IT!**

Start by opening these six cases:

The bank offer is:

If **NO DEAL**, continue by opening these five cases:

The bank offer is:

If **NO DEAL**, continue by opening these four cases:

The bank offer is:

If **NO DEAL**, continue by opening these three cases:

The bank offer is:

If **NO DEAL**, continue by opening these two cases:

The bank offer is:

DEAL or **NO DEAL**

If **NO DEAL**, continue by opening this case:

The bank offer is: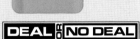

DEAL or **NO DEAL**

If **NO DEAL**, continue by opening this case:

The bank offer is:

DEAL or **NO DEAL**

If **NO DEAL**, continue by opening this case:

The bank offer is:

DEAL or **NO DEAL**

If **NO DEAL**, continue by opening this case:

The bank offer is:

DEAL or **NO DEAL**

If **NO DEAL**, there are just two cases left. You can keep your original case or switch to the one at right. Choose one and open it.

DEAL or NO DEAL

$	.01	$	1,000
$	1	$	5,000
$	5	$	10,000
$	10	$	25,000
$	25	$	50,000
$	50	$	75,000
$	75	$	100,000
$	100	$	200,000
$	200	$	300,000
$	300	$	400,000
$	400	$	500,000
$	500	$	750,000
$	750	$	1,000,000

Here is your case: **DON'T OPEN IT!**

Start by opening these six cases:

The bank offer is:

 DEAL or NO DEAL

If **NO DEAL**, continue by opening these five cases:

The bank offer is:

 DEAL or NO DEAL

If **NO DEAL**, continue by opening these four cases:

The bank offer is:

 DEAL or NO DEAL

If **NO DEAL**, continue by opening these three cases:

The bank offer is:

 DEAL or NO DEAL

If **NO DEAL**, continue by opening these two cases:

The bank offer is:

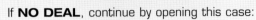

If **NO DEAL**, continue by opening this case:

The bank offer is: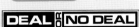

DEAL or **NO DEAL**

If **NO DEAL**, continue by opening this case:

The bank offer is:

DEAL or **NO DEAL**

If **NO DEAL**, continue by opening this case:

The bank offer is:

DEAL or **NO DEAL**

If **NO DEAL**, continue by opening this case:

The bank offer is:

DEAL or **NO DEAL**

If **NO DEAL**, there are just two cases left. You can keep your original case or switch to the one at right. Choose one and open it.

DEAL or NO DEAL	
$ .01	$ 1,000
$ 1	$ 5,000
$ 5	$ 10,000
$ 10	$ 25,000
$ 25	$ 50,000
$ 50	$ 75,000
$ 75	$ 100,000
$ 100	$ 200,000
$ 200	$ 300,000
$ 300	$ 400,000
$ 400	$ 500,000
$ 500	$ 750,000
$ 750	$ 1,000,000

Here is your case: **DON'T OPEN IT!**

Start by opening these six cases:

The bank offer is:  **DEAL** or **NO DEAL**

If **NO DEAL**, continue by opening these five cases:

The bank offer is: **DEAL** or **NO DEAL**

If **NO DEAL**, continue by opening these four cases:

The bank offer is:  **DEAL** or **NO DEAL**

If **NO DEAL**, continue by opening these three cases:

The bank offer is:  **DEAL** or **NO DEAL**

If **NO DEAL**, continue by opening these two cases:

The bank offer is:

DEAL or **NO DEAL**

If **NO DEAL**, continue by opening this case:

The bank offer is: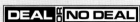

DEAL or **NO DEAL**

If **NO DEAL**, continue by opening this case:

The bank offer is: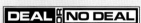

DEAL or **NO DEAL**

If **NO DEAL**, continue by opening this case:

The bank offer is: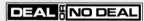

DEAL or **NO DEAL**

If **NO DEAL**, continue by opening this case:

The bank offer is: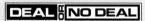

DEAL or **NO DEAL**

If **NO DEAL**, there are just two cases left. You can keep your original case or switch to the one at right. Choose one and open it.

DEAL or **NO DEAL**	
$ .01	$ 1,000
$ 1	$ 5,000
$ 5	$ 10,000
$ 10	$ 25,000
$ 25	$ 50,000
$ 50	$ 75,000
$ 75	$ 100,000
$ 100	$ 200,000
$ 200	$ 300,000
$ 300	$ 400,000
$ 400	$ 500,000
$ 500	$ 750,000
$ 750	$ 1,000,000

Here is your case: **DON'T OPEN IT!**

Start by opening these six cases:

The bank offer is:

If **NO DEAL**, continue by opening these five cases:

The bank offer is:

If **NO DEAL**, continue by opening these four cases:

The bank offer is:

If **NO DEAL**, continue by opening these three cases:

The bank offer is:

If **NO DEAL**, continue by opening these two cases:

The bank offer is: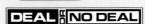

DEAL or **NO DEAL**

If **NO DEAL**, continue by opening this case: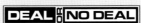

The bank offer is:

DEAL or **NO DEAL**

If **NO DEAL**, continue by opening this case: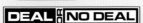

The bank offer is:

DEAL or **NO DEAL**

If **NO DEAL**, continue by opening this case:

The bank offer is:

DEAL or **NO DEAL**

If **NO DEAL**, continue by opening this case:

The bank offer is:

DEAL or **NO DEAL**

If **NO DEAL**, there are just two cases left. You can keep your original case or switch to the one at right. Choose one and open it.

DEAL or	NO DEAL
$ .01	$ 1,000
$ 1	$ 5,000
$ 5	$ 10,000
$ 10	$ 25,000
$ 25	$ 50,000
$ 50	$ 75,000
$ 75	$ 100,000
$ 100	$ 200,000
$ 200	$ 300,000
$ 300	$ 400,000
$ 400	$ 500,000
$ 500	$ 750,000
$ 750	$ 1,000,000

DEAL OR NO DEAL

$	.01	$	1,000
$	1	$	5,000
$	5	$	10,000
$	10	$	25,000
$	25	$	50,000
$	50	$	75,000
$	75	$	100,000
$	100	$	200,000
$	200	$	300,000
$	300	$	400,000
$	400	$	500,000
$	500	$	750,000
$	750	$	1,000,000